Editor

Mary S. Jones

Managing Editor

Karen J. Goldfluss, M.S. Ed.

Illustrator

Mark Mason

Cover Artist

Barb Lorseyedi

Art Production Manager

Kevin Barnes

Art Coordinator

Renée Christine Yates

Imaging

James Edward Grace
Ricardo A. Martinez

Publisher

Mary D. Smith, M.S. Ed.

Puzzles

GRADE 2

Author

Mary Rosenberg

Teacher Created Resources, Inc.

6421 Industry Way

Westminster, CA 92683

www.teachercreated.com

ISBN: 978-1-4206-3907-0

©2006 Teacher Created Resources, Inc.

Reprinted, 2011

Made in U.S.A.

The classroom teacher may reproduce copies of the materials in this book for use in a single classroom only. The reproduction of any part of the book for other classrooms or for an entire school or school system is strictly prohibited. No part of this publication may be transmitted, stored, or recorded in any form without written permission from the publisher.

Table of Contents

Introduction

The old adage "practice makes perfect" can really hold true for your child and his or her education. The more practice and exposure your child has with concepts being taught in school, the more success he or she is likely to find. For many parents, knowing how to help your children can be frustrating because the resources may not be readily available. As a parent it is also difficult to know where to focus your efforts so that the extra practice your child receives at home supports what he or she is learning in school.

This book has been designed to help both parents and teachers reinforce basic math skills. *Practice Makes Perfect* reviews basic math skills for children in grade 2. This book contains math picture puzzles that allow children to learn, review, and reinforce basic math concepts. While it would be impossible to include all concepts taught in grade 2 in this book, the following main objectives are reinforced through practice exercises:

- addition
- calendar days
- comparing numbers
- fractions
- missing addends
- multiplication

- odd & even numbers
- patterns
- place value
- rounding numbers
- subtraction

There are 38 picture puzzles organized sequentially, so children can build their knowledge from more basic skills to higher-level math skills. Math picture puzzles are designed for students to review math concepts and have fun practicing them.

How to Make the Most of This Book

Here are some useful ideas for optimizing the practice pages in this book:

- Set aside a specific place in your home to work on the practice pages. Keep it neat and tidy with materials on hand.

- Set up a certain time of day to work on the puzzles. This will establish consistency. An alternative is to look for times in your day or week that are less hectic and conducive to practicing skills.

- Keep all practice sessions with your child positive and constructive. If the mood becomes tense, or you and your child are frustrated, set the book aside and look for another time to practice with your child.

- Help with instructions if necessary. If your child is having difficulty understanding what to do or how to get started, work through the first problem with him or her.

- Review the work your child has done. This serves as reinforcement and provides further practice.

- Pay attention to the areas in which your child has the most difficulty. Provide extra guidance and exercises in those areas. Allowing children to use drawings and manipulatives, such as coins, tiles, or flash cards, can help them grasp difficult concepts more easily.

- Look for ways to make real-life applications to the skills being reinforced.

Puzzle 1

Round 'em Up!

Solve each addition problem. Color the puzzle.

6 = green   7 = blue   8 = red   9 = yellow   10 = brown

Puzzle 2

Gobble, Gobble, Gobble

Solve each addition problem. Color the puzzle.

| 10 = green   11 = brown   12 = yellow   13 = red   14 = orange |

Puzzle 3

Fly Away with Me!

Solve each addition problem. Color the puzzle.

| 15 = green | 16 = purple | 17 = yellow | 18 = red | 19 = orange | 20 = black |

Puzzle 4

Sugar Dreams

Solve each subtraction problem. Color the puzzle.

| 6 = red   7 = green   8 = pink   9 = orange   10 = purple |

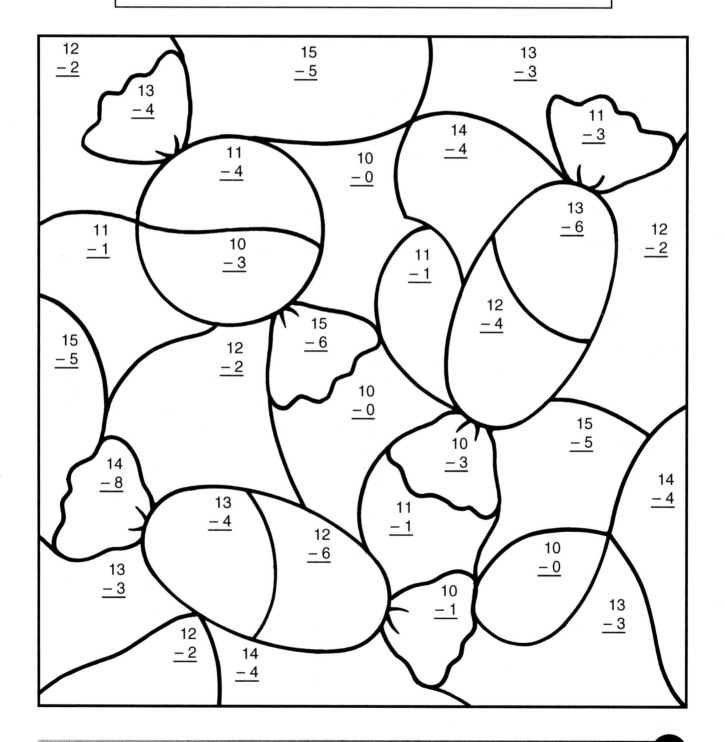

Puzzle 5 ❧ ❧ ❧ ❧ ❧ ❧ ❧ ❧ ❧ ❧ ❧ ❧ ❧

Teamwork

Solve each subtraction problem. Color the puzzle.

| 11 = red   12 = blue   13 = green   14 = purple   15 = yellow |

Puzzle 6

Let's Go Swimming

Solve each subtraction problem. Color the puzzle.

| 16 = orange | 17 = yellow | 18 = blue | 19 = green | 20 = purple |

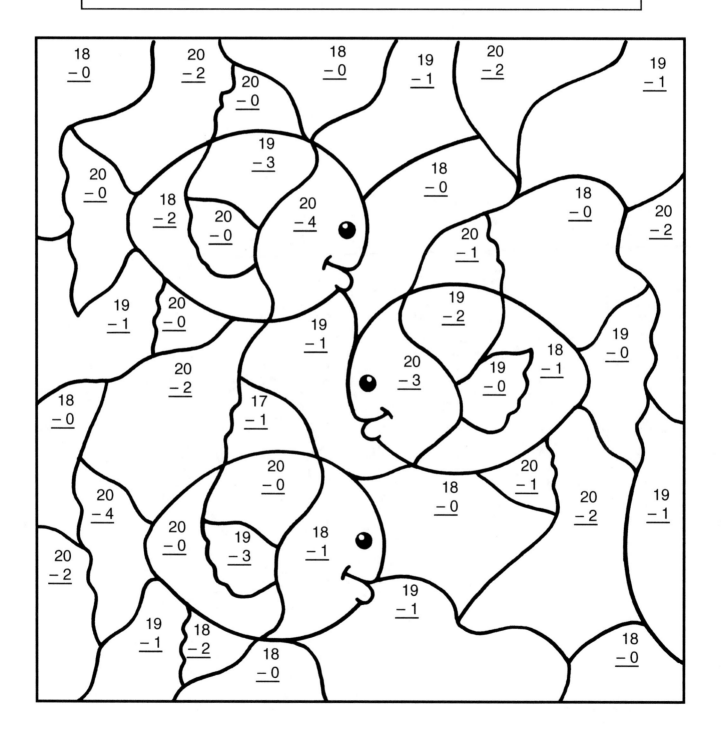

Puzzle 7

Add 'em Up!

Solve each addition problem. Color the puzzle.

| 11 = pink   12 = yellow   13 = brown   14 = gray   15 = blue |

Puzzle 8

Ribbit! Ribbit! What's Missing?

Find the missing number in each addition problem. Color the puzzle.

8 = green   9 = yellow   10 = blue

_____ + 4 = 14

1 + _____ = 11

9 + _____ = 19

2
+ _____
12

_____ = 9

3 + _____ = 13

_____ + 7 = 16

2 + _____ = 10

_____ + 11 = 20

+ 6
16

6 + _____ = 16

1 + _____

7 + _____ = 17

10
+ _____
20

12 + _____ = 20

3
+ _____
11

7
+ _____
15

9 + _____ = 17

+ 3
13

_____ + 4 = 12

6
+ _____
14

+ 8 = 16

+ 5
13

5 + _____ = 14

2
+ _____
11

10 + _____ = 18

_____ + 2 = 12

4
+ _____
14

+ 8
18

5 + _____ = 15

_____ + 1 = 11

Puzzle 9

Keep It Balanced!

Find the missing number that will make both sides of the number sentence true. Color the puzzle.

5 = blue   6 = green   7 = yellow   8 = red   9 = brown

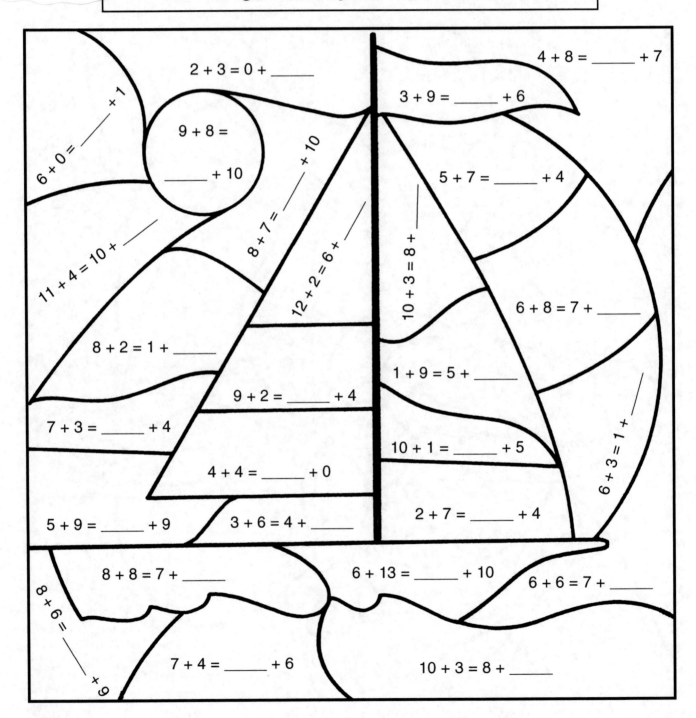

Within the puzzle image:

$4 + 8 = \underline{\qquad} + 7$

$2 + 3 = 0 + \underline{\qquad}$

$3 + 9 = \underline{\qquad} + 6$

$6 + 0 = \underline{\qquad} + 1$

$9 + 8 = \underline{\qquad} + 10$

$5 + 7 = \underline{\qquad} + 4$

$8 + 7 = \underline{\qquad} + 10$

$11 + 4 = 10 + \underline{\qquad}$

$12 + 2 = 6 + \underline{\qquad}$

$10 + 3 = 8 + \underline{\qquad}$

$6 + 8 = 7 + \underline{\qquad}$

$8 + 2 = 1 + \underline{\qquad}$

$1 + 9 = 5 + \underline{\qquad}$

$9 + 2 = \underline{\qquad} + 4$

$7 + 3 = \underline{\qquad} + 4$

$6 + 3 = 1 + \underline{\qquad}$

$10 + 1 = \underline{\qquad} + 5$

$4 + 4 = \underline{\qquad} + 0$

$5 + 9 = \underline{\qquad} + 9$

$3 + 6 = 4 + \underline{\qquad}$

$2 + 7 = \underline{\qquad} + 4$

$8 + 8 = 7 + \underline{\qquad}$

$6 + 13 = \underline{\qquad} + 10$

$6 + 6 = 7 + \underline{\qquad}$

$8 + 6 = \underline{\qquad} + 9$

$7 + 4 = \underline{\qquad} + 6$

$10 + 3 = 8 + \underline{\qquad}$

Puzzle 10

Even or Odd

Decide which numbers are even and odd. Color the puzzle.

even = brown   odd = red

Puzzle 11

Compare the Magic Dragon

Decide which numbers are greater than (>), less than (<), or equal (=) to 25. Color the puzzle.

> **(>) 25 = green   (<) 25 = yellow   (=) 25 = red**

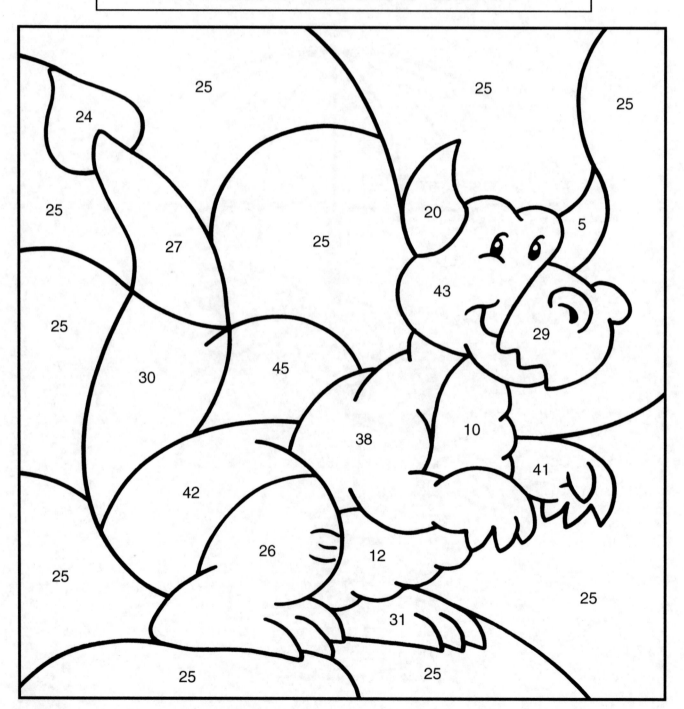

        © *Teacher Created Resources, Inc.*

Puzzle 12

Have Fun Comparing Numbers!

Decide which numbers are greater than (>), less than (<), or equal (=) to 57. Color the puzzle.

> (>) 57 = blue   (<) 57 = yellow   (=) 57 = red

Puzzle 13

Old Mac Donald

Solve each addition problem. Color the puzzle.

| 25 = brown | 26 = red | 27 = blue | 28 = yellow |

Puzzle 14

Sweet Dreams

Solve each subtraction problem. Color the puzzle.

31 = brown	32 = gray	33 = yellow	34 = red

Puzzle 15

On Fire for Subtraction!

Solve each subtraction problem. Color the puzzle.

27 = brown   28 = black   29 = gray   30 = yellow   31 = red

Puzzle 16

Row, Row, Using Tens

Solve each problem. Color the puzzle.

10 = brown	20 = black	30 = orange	40 = blue	50 = green

Puzzle 17

Buggy for Tens!

Solve each problem. Color the puzzle.

60 = yellow	70 = orange	80 = green	90 = black	100 = red

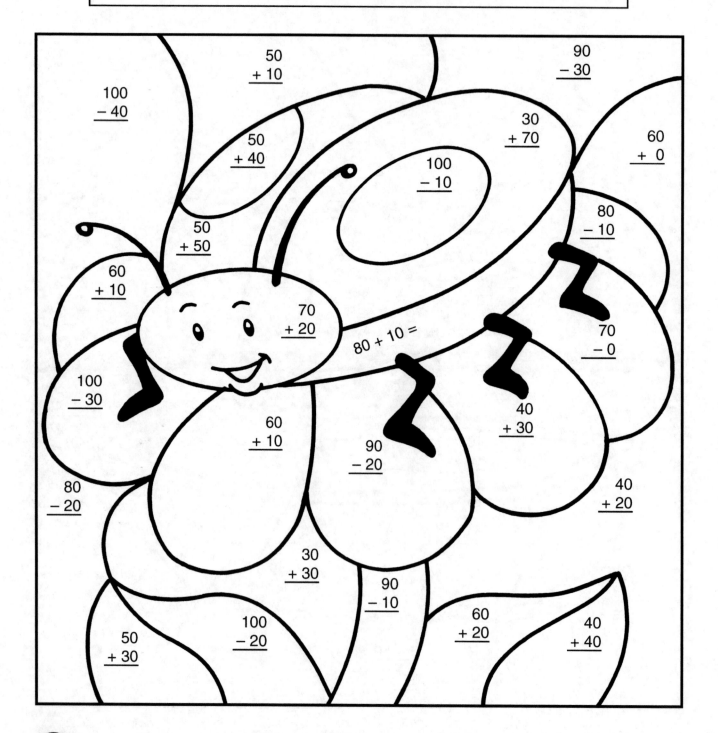

Puzzle 18

Adding Together

Solve each addition problem. Color the puzzle.

| 25 = brown | 26 = green | 27 = yellow | 28 = blue | 29 = purple |

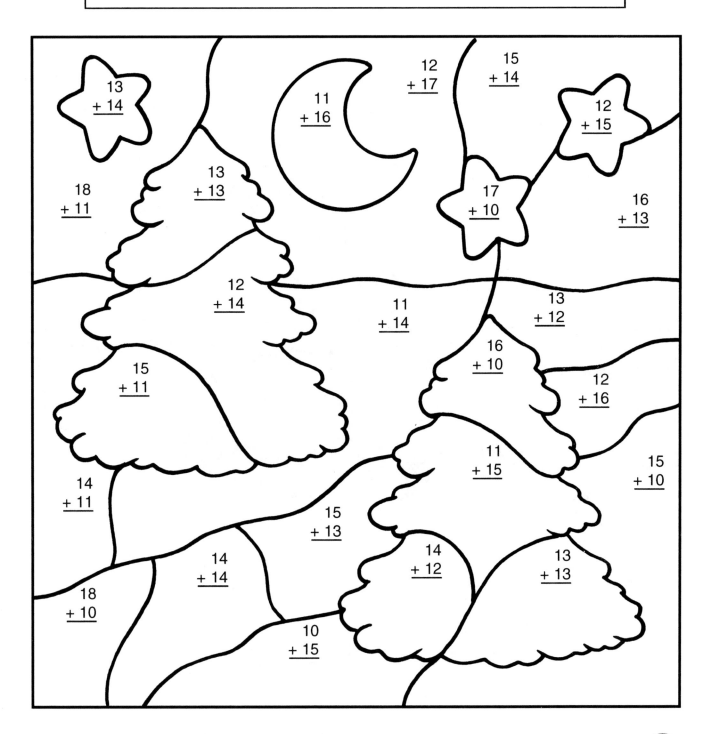

Puzzle 19 🌀 🌀 🌀 🌀 🌀 🌀 🌀 🌀 🌀 🌀 🌀 🌀

Reporting for Duty!

Solve each addition problem. Color the puzzle.

| **35 = gray** | **36 = green** | **37 = brown** | **38 = black** | **39 = yellow** |

Addition

Puzzle 20

A Dog's Life

Solve each addition problem. Color the puzzle.

45 = red	46 = brown	47 = yellow	48 = green	49 = black

Puzzle 21

I'm the Boss!

Solve each addition problem. Color the puzzle.

55 = gray	56 = white	57 = pink	58 = brown	59 = red

Puzzle 22

Ahhh! This is the Life!

Solve each addition problem. Color the puzzle.

65 = green	66 = brown	67 = orange	68 = yellow	69 = blue

Subtraction

Puzzle 23

What's for Dinner?

Solve each subtraction problem. Color the puzzle.

0 = yellow   1 = gray   2 = brown   3 = red

© Teacher Created Resources, Inc.

Puzzle 24

Shell Subtraction

Solve each subtraction problem. Color the puzzle.

7 = blue   8 = brown   9 = yellow   10 = pink

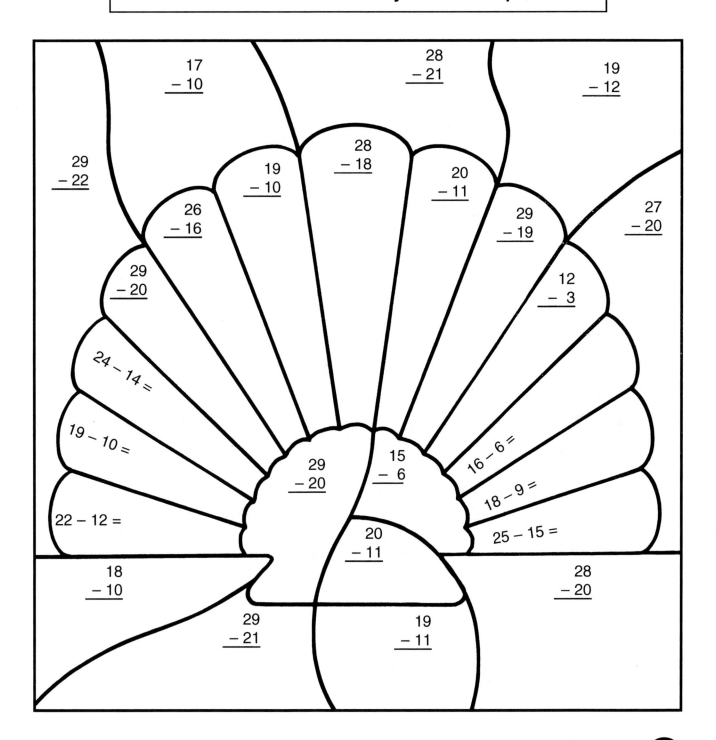

Puzzle 25

Howdy!

Solve each subtraction problem. Color the puzzle.

4 = brown   5 = green   6 = blue   7 = red   8 = yellow

© *Teacher Created Resources, Inc.*

Subtraction

Puzzle 26

Try It! It's Good for You!

Solve each subtraction problem. Color the puzzle.

58 = pink   59 = gray   60 = brown   61 = green   62 = blue

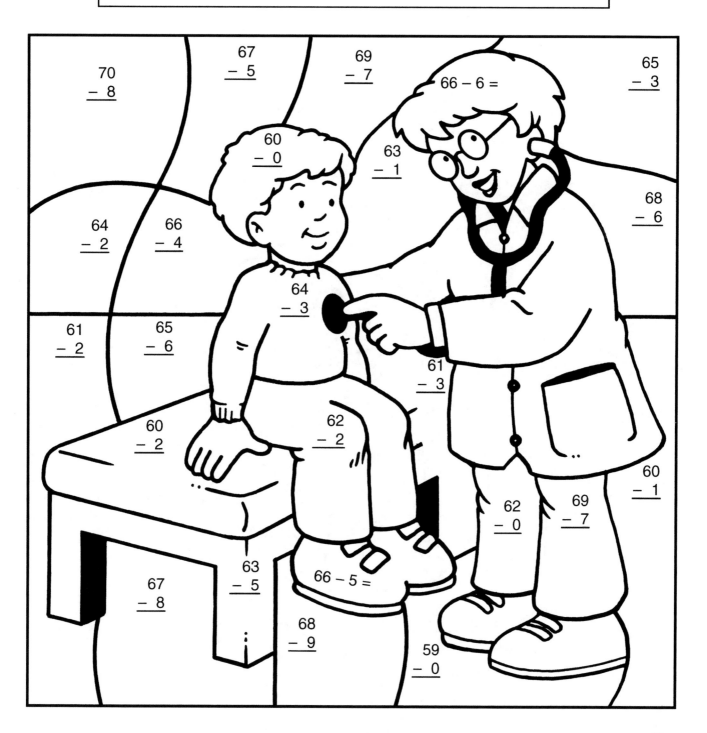

Puzzle 27

Toss It Up!

Solve each problem. Color the puzzle.

25 = brown	26 = blue	27 = yellow	28 = gray	29 = green	30 = red

Puzzle 28

Let's Ride!

Solve each problem. Color the puzzle.

41 = yellow	42 = green	43 = brown	44 = purple	45 = red

Puzzle 29

Pierre the Artist

Solve each problem. Color the puzzle.

| 73 = brown | 74 = purple | 75 = red | 76 = yellow | 77 = green |

Puzzle 30

Calendar Days

Decide what type of day is labeled. Color the puzzle.

day of the week = green   year = blue
month of the year = yellow   holiday = red

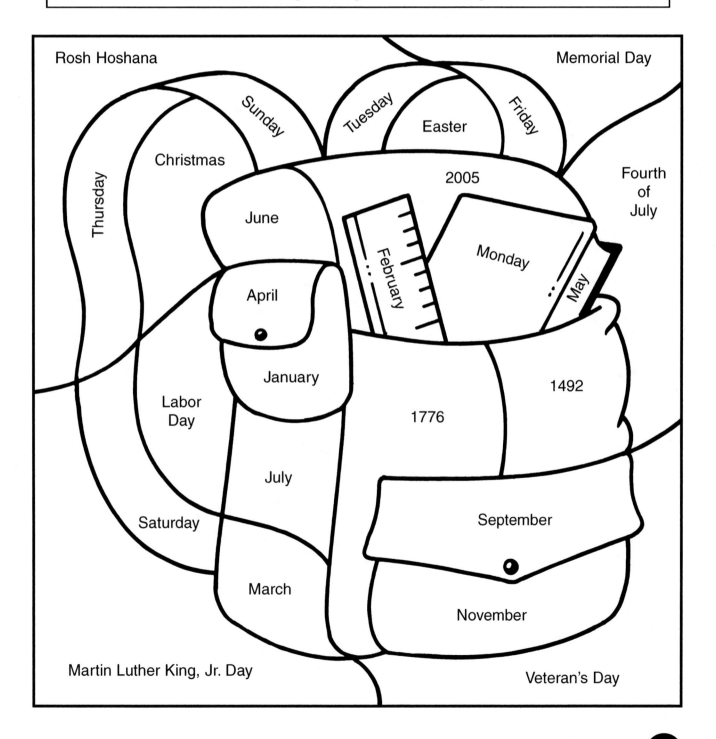

Puzzle 31 🐚 🐚 🐚 🐚 🐚 🐚 🐚 🐚 🐚 🐚 🐚 🐚 🐚 🐚

What's the Fraction?

Identify the fraction. Color the puzzle.

| halves = red | thirds = blue | quarters = yellow | fifths = green |

Puzzle 32

What's Missing?

Complete each number pattern. Color the puzzle.

> **86 = pink   87 = yellow   88 = blue   89 = green   90 = orange**

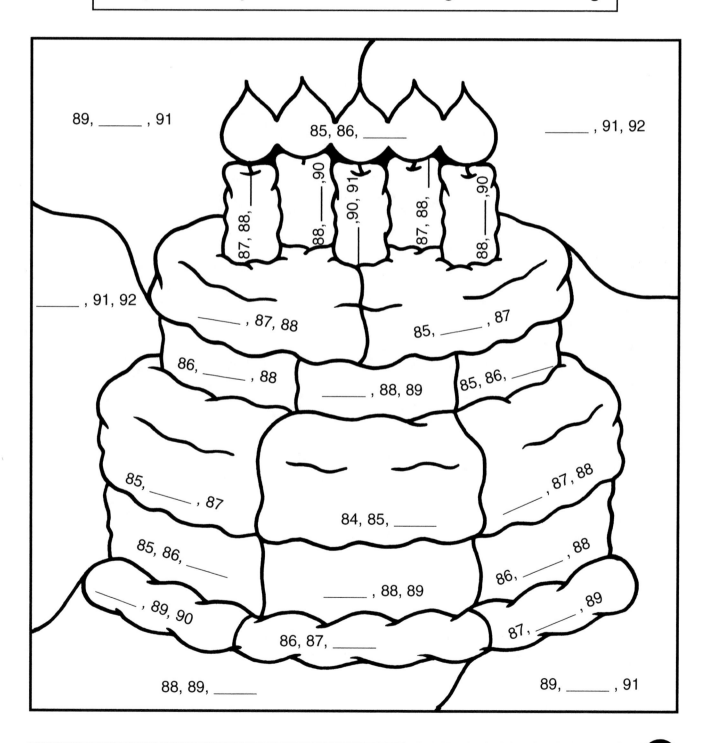

Puzzle 33

Rounding Around

Round each number to the nearest ten. Color the puzzle.

| 10 = red | 20 = green | 30 = yellow | 40 = purple |

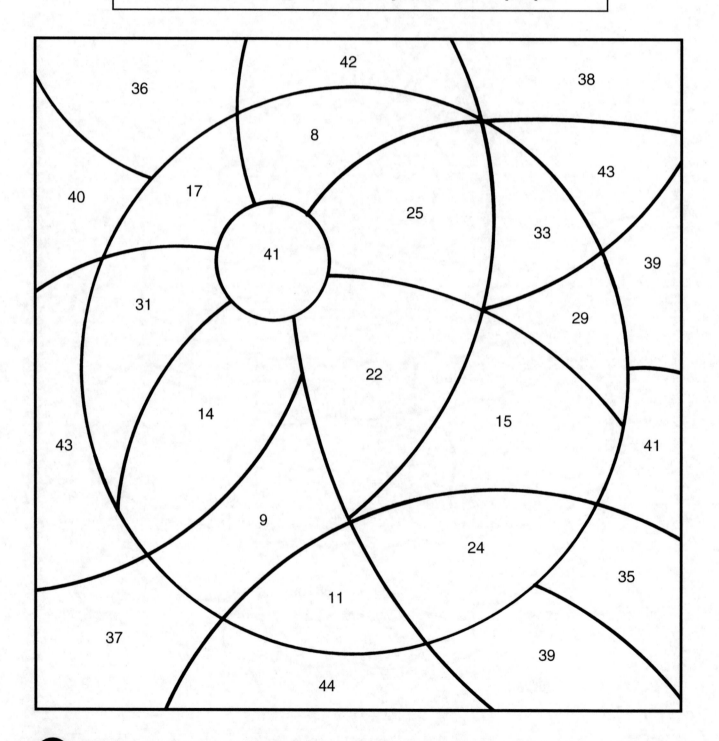

  © *Teacher Created Resources, Inc.*

Puzzle 34

Tens and Ones

Identify each value. Color the puzzle.

| 1 one = yellow   2 ones = green   3 tens = blue   4 tens = purple |

Puzzle 35

One to One Hundred

Identify each value. Color the puzzle.

| 0 ones = black 2 ones = red 3 tens = green 4 tens = yellow |
| 8 hundreds = pink 9 hundreds = purple |

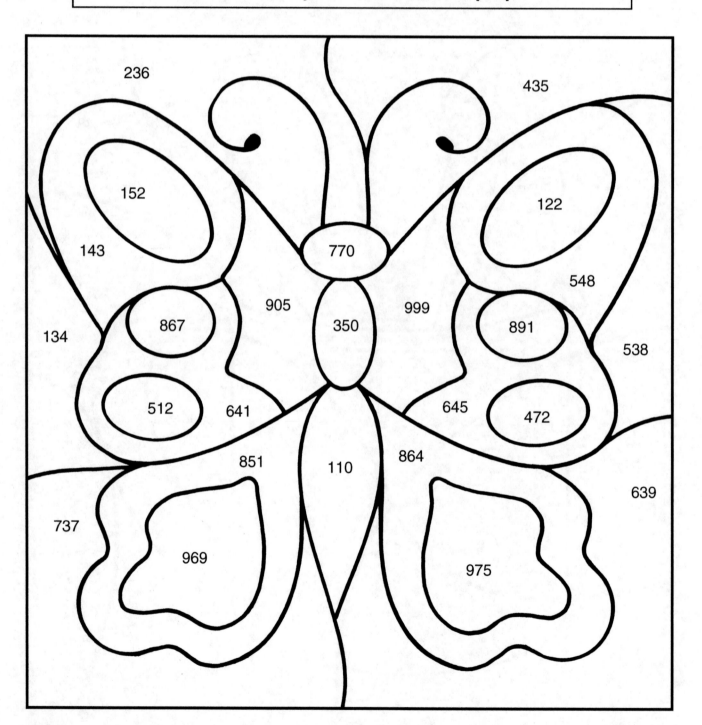

Puzzle 36

Happy Days!

Identify each value. Color the puzzle.

2 ones = green	3 tens = blue	4 hundreds = yellow	1 thousand = brown

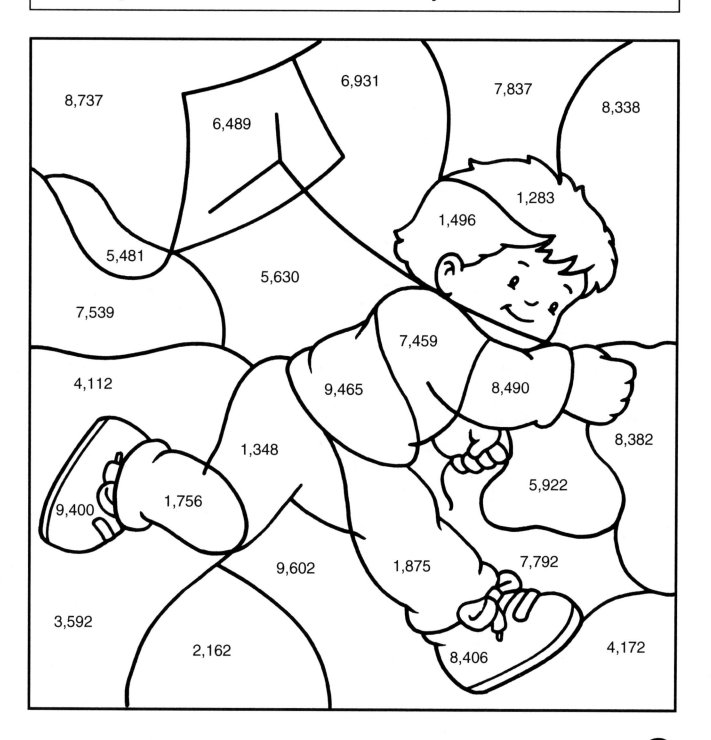

Puzzle 37

Beginning to Multiply

Solve each multiplication problem. Color the puzzle.

| 2 = red | 4 = yellow | 6 = green | 8 = blue | 10 = orange | 12 = purple |

Puzzle 38

More Multiplication Fun

Solve each multiplication problem. Color the puzzle.

3 = red   6 = blue   9 = yellow   12 = green   15 = purple

Answer Key

Puzzle 1 Page 4

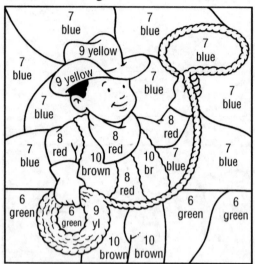

Puzzle 2 Page 5

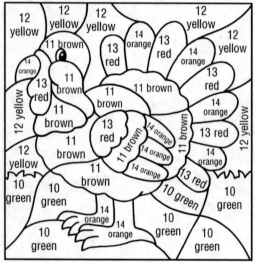

Puzzle 3 Page 6

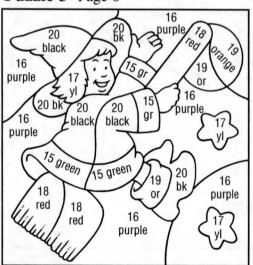

Puzzle 4 Page 7

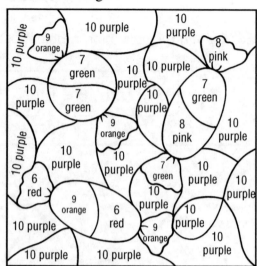

Puzzle 5 Page 8

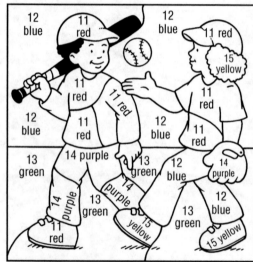

Puzzle 6 Page 9

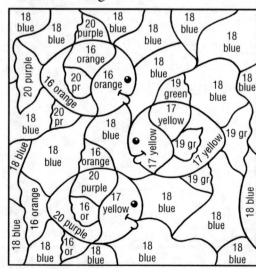

#3907 Practice Makes Perfect: Math Picture Puzzles   © *Teacher Created Resources, Inc.*

Answer Key ♪ ✿ ♪ ✿ ♪ ✿ ♪ ✿ ♪ ✿ ♪ ✿ ♪ ✿

Puzzle 7 Page 10

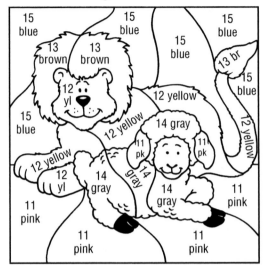

Puzzle 8 Page 11

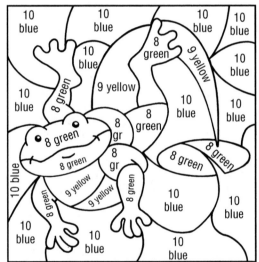

Puzzle 9 Page 12

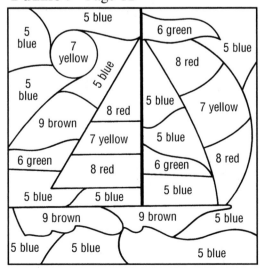

Puzzle 10 Page 13

Puzzle 11 Page 14

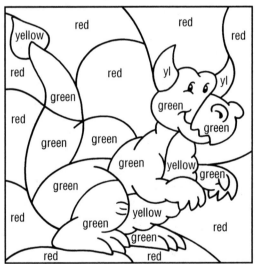

Puzzle 12 Page 15

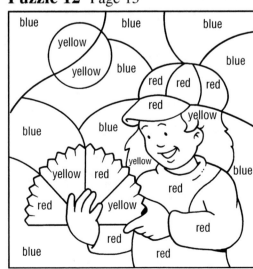

Answer Key ❧ ❧ ❧ ❧ ❧ ❧ ❧ ❧ ❧ ❧ ❧ ❧ ❧

Puzzle 13 Page 16

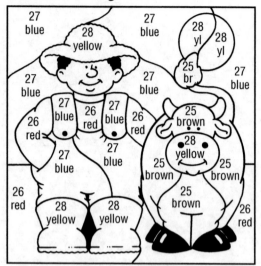

Puzzle 14 Page 17

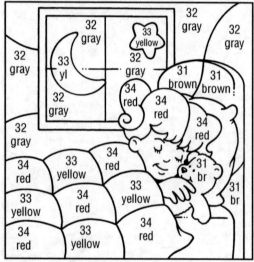

Puzzle 15 Page 18

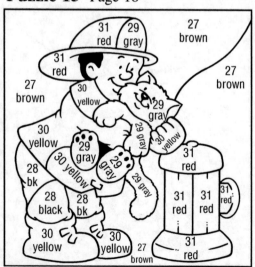

Puzzle 16 Page 19

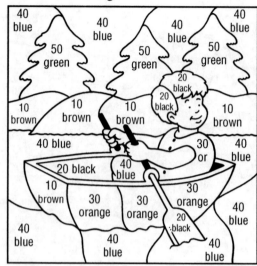

Puzzle 17 Page 20

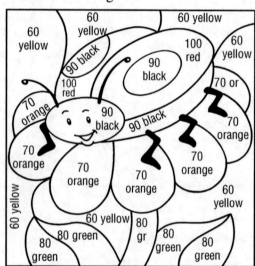

Puzzle 18 Page 21

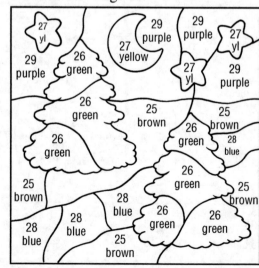

Answer Key

Puzzle 19 Page 22

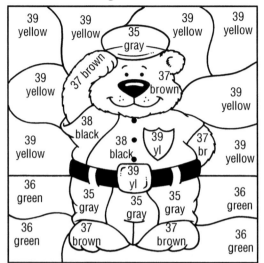

Puzzle 22 Page 25

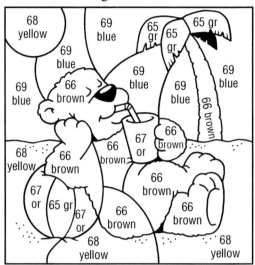

Puzzle 20 Page 23

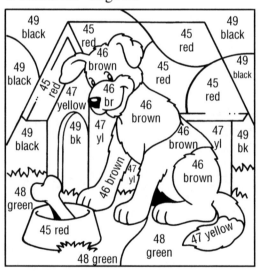

Puzzle 23 Page 26

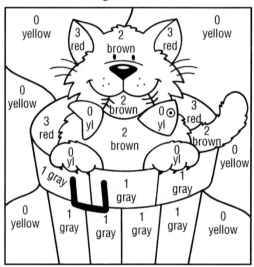

Puzzle 21 Page 24

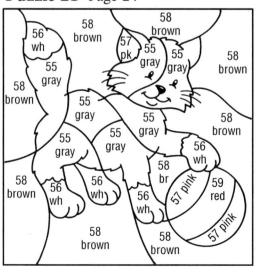

Puzzle 24 Page 27

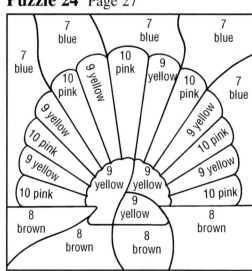

Answer Key ♪ ☙ ♪ ☙ ♪ ☙ ♪ ☙ ♪ ☙ ♪ ♪ ☙ ♪ ☙

Puzzle 25 Page 28

Puzzle 28 Page 31

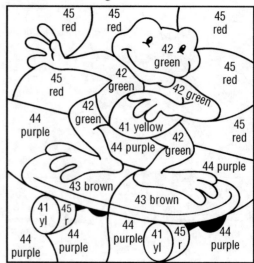

Puzzle 26 Page 29

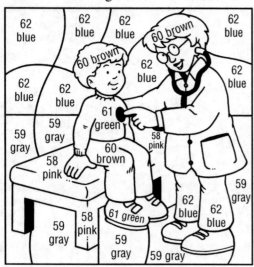

Puzzle 29 Page 32

Puzzle 27 Page 30

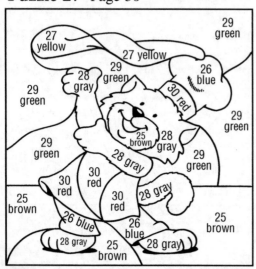

Puzzle 30 Page 33

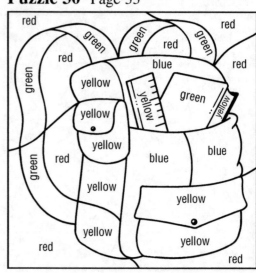

#3907 Practice Makes Perfect: Math Picture Puzzles

© Teacher Created Resources, Inc.

Answer Key

Puzzle 31 Page 34

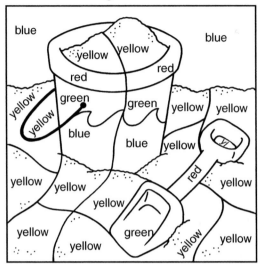

Puzzle 32 Page 35

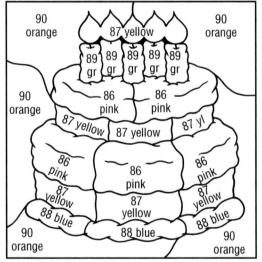

Puzzle 33 Page 36

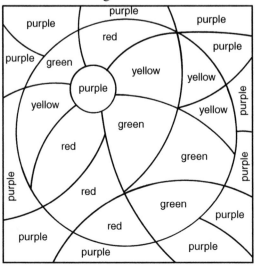

Puzzle 34 Page 37

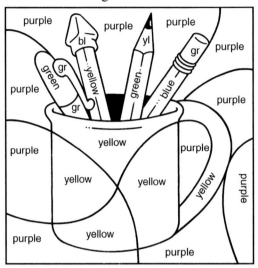

Puzzle 35 Page 38

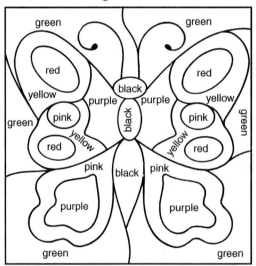

Puzzle 36 Page 39

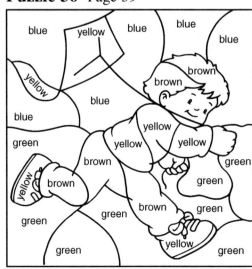

© Teacher Created Resources, Inc. *#3907 Practice Makes Perfect: Math Picture Puzzles*

Answer Key

Puzzle 37 Page 40

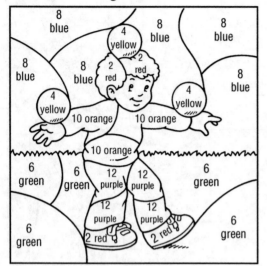

Puzzle 38 Page 41

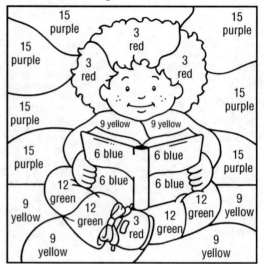

#3907 Practice Makes Perfect: Math Picture Puzzles   © Teacher Created Resources, Inc.